Soufflé

A Delicious Collection of Sweet and Savory Soufflé Recipes

By
BookSumo Press
All rights reserved

Published by
http://www.booksumo.com

ENJOY THE RECIPES?
KEEP ON COOKING WITH 6 MORE FREE COOKBOOKS!

Visit our website and simply enter your email address to join the club and receive your 6 cookbooks.

http://booksumo.com/magnet

https://www.instagram.com/booksumopress/

https://www.facebook.com/booksumo/

LEGAL NOTES

All Rights Reserved. No Part Of This Book May Be Reproduced Or Transmitted In Any Form Or By Any Means. Photocopying, Posting Online, And / Or Digital Copying Is Strictly Prohibited Unless Written Permission Is Granted By The Book's Publishing Company. Limited Use Of The Book's Text Is Permitted For Use In Reviews Written For The Public.

Table of Contents

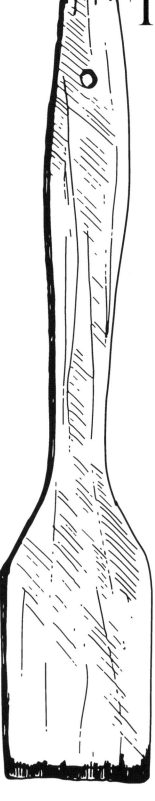

Creamy Sour Corn Soufflé 7

Easter Soufflé 8

Flapjack Soufflé 9

November's Soufflé 10

Nebraska Fish Soufflé 11

German Soufflé 12

Sweet French Bread Soufflé 13

American Gratin Soufflé 14

Bittersweet Soufflé 15

Soufflé Mornings 16

Cheddar Squash Soufflé 17

Tomato & Chives Soufflé 18

Citrus Pastry Soufflé 19

Carolina Grits Soufflé 20

Crab & Egg Soufflé 21

Minced Rice Soufflé 22

Ketogenic Soufflé 23

Soufflé Bites 24

Swiss Chocolate Soufflé 26

Chinese Soufflé 28

Soufflé in its Simplest 29

Chipotle Soufflé 30

Maple Soufflé 31

Big Apple Soufflé 32

Western European Soufflé 33

Brazilian Fruit Soufflé 34

How to Make a Soufflé 35

Mint Cocoa Soufflé 36

Sweet Ricotta Soufflé 38

Dry Mustard Soufflé 39

Spicy Bell Mushroom Soufflé 40

Authentic Vegan Soufflé 41

Burrito Soufflé 42

Crab & Coconut Soufflé 43

Cheesy Herb Soufflé 45

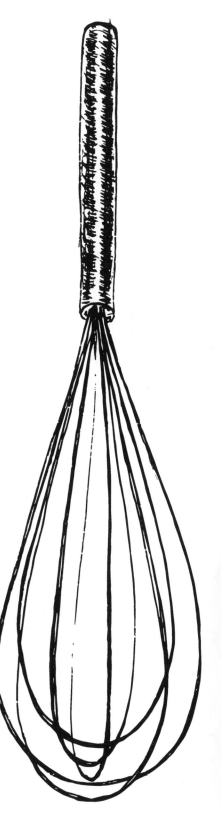

Potato Soufflé 46

Mac & Cheese Soufflé 47

Lemony Raspberry Soufflé 48

Pepperoni & Cheese Soufflé 49

Milky Asparagus Soufflé 50

Pumpkin Soufflé 51

Nutty Pecan Soufflé 52

Carrot Soufflé 53

Creamy Sour Corn Soufflé

🍳 Prep Time: 10 mins
🕐 Total Time: 45 mins

Servings per Recipe: 4
Calories   235.1
Fat   10.0g
Cholesterol   122.6mg
Sodium   517.3mg
Carbohydrates   32.3g
Protein   6.9g

Ingredients

- 2 eggs
- 2 tbsp cornstarch
- 2 tbsp sugar
- 1/4 tsp salt
- 1/8 tsp pepper
- 1 dash nutmeg
- 1 (14-16 oz.) cans creamed corn
- 1/2 C. sour cream
- 1/2 C. milk

Directions

1. Set your oven to 400 degrees F before doing anything else and arrange a rack in the center of oven. Grease an 8-inch square baking dish.
2. In a bowl, crack the eggs and with an electric mixer, beat until foamy.
3. Add the remaining ingredients and beat until well combined.
4. Place the mixture into prepared baking dish.
5. Cook in the oven for about 35 minutes or till a toothpick inserted in the center comes out clean.

EASTER
Soufflé

🥣 Prep Time: 1 hr
🕒 Total Time: 2 hrs 10 mins

Servings per Recipe: 6
Calories 433.7
Fat 18.0g
Cholesterol 133.6mg
Sodium 340.3mg
Carbohydrates 65.6g
Protein 4.9g

Ingredients

1 1/2 lb. carrots, sliced
1/2 C. butter
3 eggs
1 tsp vanilla
1/4 C. all-purpose flour

1 1/2 tsp baking powder
1 1/2 C. sugar
3/4 tsp ground cinnamon

Directions

1. Set your oven to 350 degrees F before doing anything else and lightly, grease 1 1/2-quart soufflé dish.
2. In a pan of water, add carrots and bring to a boil.
3. Cook for about 20-25 minutes. Drain well.
4. In a food processor, add the coked carrots and remaining ingredients and pulse
5. until smooth.
6. Transfer the mixture into the prepared soufflé dish evenly.
7. Cook in the oven for about 1 hour and 10 minutes.

Flapjack Soufflé

Prep Time: 10 mins
Total Time: 30 mins

Servings per Recipe: 8
Calories   243.4
Fat   16.0g
Cholesterol   152.0mg
Sodium   164.7mg
Carbohydrates   16.9g
Protein   7.3g

Ingredients

1/2 C. butter
5 eggs
1 1/4 C. milk
1 1/4 C. all-purpose flour
1 tsp vanilla

Directions

1. Set your oven to 425 degrees F before doing anything else.
2. In the bottom of 9X13-inch baking dish, add the butter and place in the oven to melt, while preheating.
3. In a blender, add eggs and pulse until beaten.
4. Add the milk, flour and vanilla extract and pulse for about 30 seconds.
5. Place the mixture into the baking dish with melted butter.
6. Cook in the oven for about 20 minutes.

NOVEMBER'S
Soufflé

Prep Time: 10 mins
Total Time: 45 mins

Servings per Recipe: 8
Calories   429.8
Fat   19.3g
Cholesterol   75.3mg
Sodium   263.2mg
Carbohydrates   62.2g
Protein   4.7g

Ingredients

3 C. sweet potatoes, mashed (canned)
3/4 C. sugar
1/2 tsp salt
2 eggs
1/4 C. butter
1/2 C. milk
1 tsp vanilla

Garnish
1 C. brown sugar
1 C. chopped pecans
1/3 C. flour
1/4 C. butter, melted

Directions

1. Set your oven to 350 degrees F before doing anything else and grease a 9x2-inch round baking dish.
2. In a bowl, add the sweet potatoes, sugar, salt, eggs 1/4 C. of the butter, milk and vanilla and mix until well combined.
3. For topping: in another bowl, add all ingredients and mix well.
4. Place the sweet potato mixture into the prepared baking dish evenly and sprinkle with topping mixture.
5. Cook in the oven for about 35 minutes.

Nebraska Fish Soufflé

Prep Time: 15 mins
Total Time: 40 mins

Servings per Recipe: 4
Calories   244.3
Fat   16.3g
Cholesterol   190.4mg
Sodium   772.5mg
Carbohydrates   7.5g
Protein   16.1g

Ingredients

- 3 tbsp butter
- 3 tbsp flour
- 1 C. milk
- 1 tsp salt
- pepper (to taste)
- 1 (6 oz.) cans salmon, flaked and bones crushed
- 3 eggs, separated

Directions

1. Set your oven to 350 degrees F before doing anything else and grease a soufflé dish.
2. In a small pan, melt the butter and stir in the milk, flour, salt and pepper until well combined.
3. Cook until the mixture becomes thick.
4. Meanwhile, in a small bowl, add the egg yolks and beat slightly.
5. Remove from heat and stir in the salmon and egg yolks.
6. In a small bowl, add the egg whites and beat until stiff peaks form.
7. Place the mixture into the prepared soufflé dish evenly.
8. Cook in the oven for about 20-25 minutes.

GERMAN Soufflé

🍳 Prep Time: 20 mins
🕐 Total Time: 35 mins

Servings per Recipe: 2
Calories 674.6
Fat 57.9g
Cholesterol 214.0mg
Sodium 122.8mg
Carbohydrates 51.3g
Protein 17.6g

Ingredients

1 oz. heavy cream
4 oz. dark chocolate
1/2 tbsp butter
2 large eggs (separated into whites and yolks)
1 dash cream of tartar
1/4 C. sugar

Topping:
berries
2 pieces dark chocolate
powdered sugar

Directions

1. Set your oven to 375 degrees F before doing anything else and arrange rack in the middle of oven.
2. Grease 2 (6-oz.) ramekins with some cold butter and then, dust with some granulated sugar and cocoa powder.
3. Shake and roll each ramekin to coat the bottom and sides evenly.
4. In the double boiler, add the cream, butter and chocolate and melt, stirring frequently.
5. Remove from the heat.
6. Add the two egg yolks into the chocolate mixture and beat until well combined.
7. In a bowl, add the egg whites and cream of tartar and beat until soft peaks are formed.
8. Add the sugar and beat until stiff peaks are formed. Slowly and gently, fold whipped egg whites into the chocolate mixture.
9. Divide the mixture into the prepared ramekins about 3/4 of the way up.
10. Place a piece of chocolate or berries on top of each ramekin and gently, push into the mixture.
11. Arrange the ramekins into a baking dish and cook in the oven for about 15 minutes.
12. Remove from the oven and dust with the sugar.
13. Serve immediately with a garnishing of the berries.

Sweet French Bread Soufflé

Prep Time: 10 mins
Total Time: 1 hr 5 mins

Servings per Recipe: 12
Calories   811.5
Fat   29.0g
Cholesterol   249.5mg
Sodium   1101.2mg
Carbohydrates   108.9g
Protein   29.3g

Ingredients

- 1/2 C. butter, softened
- 8 oz. cream cheese
- 1/2 C. maple syrup
- 2 loaves French bread, cubed
- 12 eggs
- 3 C. half-and-half
- 1 1/2 tsp vanilla
- ground cinnamon, for dusting
- powdered sugar, for dusting

Directions

1. Grease 2 (7x11-inch) baking dishes with some butter.
2. Place bread cubes into prepared baking dishes about half way full.
3. In a small bowl, add the cream cheese, butter and maple syrup and mix until well combined.
4. In another large bowl, add the half-and-half, eggs and vanilla and beat until well combined.
5. Place the cream cheese mixture over bread cubes evenly, followed by the egg mixture.
6. Sprinkle with the cinnamon and refrigerate, covered overnight.
7. Set your oven to 350 degrees F.
8. Remove the baking dish from refrigerator and cook in the oven for about 55-60 minutes.
9. Remove from the oven and serve with a dusting of the powdered sugar.

AMERICAN
Gratin Soufflé

Prep Time: 25 mins
Total Time: 55 mins

Servings per Recipe: 4
Calories 297.7
Fat 18.5g
Cholesterol 127.7mg
Sodium 351.1mg
Carbohydrates 26.1g
Protein 8.2g

Ingredients

1 large eggplant, pared and cubed
2 beaten eggs
1/2 C. milk
1/2 C. dry breadcrumbs
1 C. shredded American cheese
1/4 C. melted butter
3/4 C. crushed crackers

Directions

1. Set your oven to 350 degrees F before doing anything else and grease a casserole dish.
2. In a pan of salted boiling water, cook the eggplant cubes for about 15 minutes.
3. Drain the eggplant cubes well and transfer into a a bowl.
4. With a fork, mash the eggplant cubes well.
5. Add the 3/4 C. of the cheese, milk, eggs, breadcrumbs, salt and pepper and mix until well combined.
6. In another small bowl, add the crackers and melted butter and mix well.
7. Place the eggplant mixture into the prepared casserole dish evenly and top with the cracker mixture, followed by the remaining 1/4 C. of the cheese.
8. Cook in the oven for about 30 minutes.

Bittersweet Soufflé

Prep Time: 15 mins
Total Time: 27 mins

Servings per Recipe: 12
Calories	216.4
Fat	17.7g
Cholesterol	133.6mg
Sodium	170.6mg
Carbohydrates	11.4g
Protein	3.5g

Ingredients

- 8 oz. bittersweet chocolate, chopped
- 8 oz. butter, diced
- 6 eggs
- 4 oz. sugar
- 1 oz. sifted flour
- nonstick cooking spray

Directions

1. Set your oven to 325 degrees F before doing anything else and grease 12 soufflé dishes with non-stick spray.
2. In the top of a double boiler, place the chocolate and butter and heat until melted, stirring continuously.
3. In a bowl, add the eggs and sugar and beat until light and fluffy.
4. Add the flour into the bowl of chocolate mixture and mix well
5. Gently fold the chocolate mixture into the flour mixture.
6. Place the mixture into the prepared soufflé dishes evenly.
7. Cook in the oven for about 9-12 minutes.
8. Serve immediately.

SOUFFLÉ
Mornings

Prep Time: 10 mins
Total Time: 55 mins

Servings per Recipe: 6
Calories   445.3
Fat   29.2g
Cholesterol   297.9mg
Sodium   1168.3mg
Carbohydrates   17.2g
Protein   27.0g

Ingredients

1 lb. mild bulk beef sausage
6 eggs
2 C. milk
1 tsp salt
1 tsp dry mustard
6 slices white bread (cubed)
1 C. cheddar cheese (grated)

Directions

1. Heat a skillet and cook the crumbled sausage until browned.
2. Drain the grease and keep aside to cool.
3. In a large bowl, add the eggs, add milk, dry mustard and salt and beat well.
4. Add the bread cubes and stir to combine.
5. Add the cheese and browned sausage and mix well.
6. Refrigerate, covered overnight.
7. Set your oven to 350 degrees F.
8. Cook in the oven for about 45 minutes.

Cheddar Squash Soufflé

Prep Time: 15 mins
Total Time: 1 hr 15 mins

Servings per Recipe: 4
Calories	796.3
Fat	54.4g
Cholesterol	206.9mg
Sodium	1665.3mg
Carbohydrates	52.1g
Protein	26.3g

Ingredients

- 2 lb. yellow squash, sliced
- 1 medium onion, sliced
- 1 tsp salt
- 1/2 tsp sugar
- 6 tbsp butter, melted
- 3 tbsp flour
- 2 eggs, slightly beaten
- 1 C. milk
- 1/2 lb. sharp cheddar cheese, grated
- 1/2 box crackers, crumbled

Directions

1. Set your oven to 350 degrees F before doing anything else and grease a 1 1/2-quart casserole dish.
2. In a pan, add the squash, sugar, salt, black pepper and enough water to cover and simmer for about 20 minutes.
3. Drain the squash well and transfer into a bowl.
4. With a potato masher, mash the squash well.
5. Add flour, eggs, milk, cheese and 3 tbsp of butter and mix until well combined.
6. Transfer the mixture into the prepared casserole dish.
7. Cook in the oven for about 30 minutes.
8. Meanwhile, in a bowl, mix together the remaining butter and cracker crumbs.
9. Remove the casserole dish from oven and sprinkle with the cracker crumb evenly.
10. Cook in the oven for about 10 minutes more.

TOMATO & Chives Soufflé

Prep Time: 20 mins
Total Time: 32 mins

Servings per Recipe: 4
Calories 106.5
Fat 3.8g
Cholesterol 124.5mg
Sodium 93.9mg
Carbohydrates 12.7g
Protein 6.1g

Ingredients

4 large tomatoes, halved and seeded
3 egg yolks
2 tbsp breadcrumbs
1 tbsp chives
2 egg whites, beaten

Directions

1. Set your oven to 375 degrees F before doing anything else.
2. Carefully, scoop out the pulp from each tomato half and reserve the tomato half shells.
3. Then, chop the tomato pulp very finely.
4. In a large bowl, add the chopped tomatoes, breadcrumbs and egg yolks and mix well.
5. Gently, fold in beaten egg whites.
6. Carefully, spoon the tomato pulp mixture into each tomato shell evenly.
7. Arrange filled tomato shells in a flat, oven-proof baking dish.
8. Cook in the oven for about 12 minutes.
9. Remove from the oven and serve immediately with the sprinkling of chives.

Citrus Pastry Soufflé

Prep Time: 15 mins
Total Time: 1 hr 30 mins

Servings per Recipe: 8
Calories   465.3
Fat   33.1g
Cholesterol   270.9mg
Sodium   385.4mg
Carbohydrates   27.0g
Protein   15.0g

Ingredients

Filling:
8 oz. cream cheese
15 oz. ricotta cheese
2 egg yolks
1 tbsp sugar
1 tsp vanilla
Pastry
1/2 C. butter, softened
1/3 C. sugar
6 eggs
1 C. all-purpose flour
2 tsp baking powder
1 1/2 C. Greek yogurt
1/2 C. orange juice
Garnish
fresh sweetened fruit (berries)

Directions

1. Set your oven to 350 degrees F before doing anything else and grease a 9x13x2-inch glass baking dish.
2. For the filling: in a small bowl, add the cream cheese and beat until smooth.
3. Add the egg yolks, ricotta cheese, sugar and vanilla extract and mix until well combined.
4. For blintz: in a large bowl, add the butter and sugar and beat until creamy.
5. Add eggs and beat until well combined.
6. In a third bowl, mix together the flour and baking powder.
7. In a fourth bowl, mix together the yogurt and orange juice.
8. Add alternately into the egg mixture and mix until well combined.
9. Place half of the mixture into the prepared baking dish and top with the filling mixture evenly.
10. Place the remaining mixture over the filling evenly.
11. Cook in the oven for about 45-55 minutes.
12. Remove from the oven and keep onto a wire rack to cool for about 15 minutes before cutting. Serve with fresh sweetened fruit.

CAROLINA
Grits Soufflé

Prep Time: 30 mins
Total Time: 2 hrs

Servings per Recipe: 12
Calories	273.0
Fat	18.5g
Cholesterol	102.9mg
Sodium	251.7mg
Carbohydrates	16.0g
Protein	10.4g

Ingredients

1 1/2 C. regular grits, cooked
1 tsp onion salt
1 tsp garlic salt
3/4 tsp Worcestershire sauce
1/2 C. butter
3 eggs, slightly beaten
3/4 lb. cheddar cheese, shredded
paprika

Directions

1. In a large bowl, add the cooked grits, onion salt, garlic salt, Worcestershire sauce and butter and mix until well combined.
2. Add the beaten eggs and cheese and stir combine.
3. Transfer the mixture into a 2 1/2-quart baking dish and sprinkle with the paprika generously.
4. Refrigerate, covered overnight.
5. Set your oven to 350 degrees F.
6. Remove from the refrigerator and keep aside for at least 15 minutes before baking.
7. Cook in the oven for about 1 1/2 hours.

Crab & Egg Soufflé

Prep Time: 15 mins
Total Time: 1 hr

Servings per Recipe: 6
Calories 292.7
Fat 23.8g
Cholesterol 467.4mg
Sodium 649.6mg
Carbohydrates 2.9g
Protein 16.1g

Ingredients

- 12 eggs
- 1/2 C. milk
- 1 tsp salt
- 1/2 tsp white pepper
- 1/2 tsp dried dill
- 1 C. crab
- 8 oz. cream cheese, cubed
- paprika
- butter, melted for ramekins

Directions

1. Set your oven to 350 degrees F before doing anything else and grease 6 ramekins with the melted butter.
2. In a bowl, add the milk, eggs, dill, salt and pepper and beat until well combined.
3. Add the crab and cheese and gently, stir to combine.
4. Place the mixture into the prepared ramekins evenly and sprinkle with the paprika.
5. Cook in the oven for about 40 - 45 minutes.

MINCED
Rice Soufflé

🍳 Prep Time: 20 mins
🕐 Total Time: 1 hr 5 mins

Servings per Recipe: 6
Calories   302.3
Fat   18.1g
Cholesterol   154.1mg
Sodium   472.9mg
Carbohydrates   20.4g
Protein   13.9g

Ingredients

2 tbsp butter
2 tbsp all-purpose flour
1 1/2 C. milk
2 C. cooked long-grain rice
1 1/2 C. shredded sharp cheddar cheese
1 tbsp minced green onion
1 tbsp minced fresh parsley
1/2 tsp salt
1 tsp Worcestershire sauce
1/4 tsp Tabasco sauce
3 eggs, separated

Directions

1. In a heavy pan, melt the butter over low heat and stir in the flour until smooth.
2. Cook for about 1 minute, stirring continuously.
3. Slowly, stir in the milk and cook until mixture becomes thick.
4. Add the remaining ingredients except the egg and stir to combine.
5. Remove from the heat and keep aside to cool completely.
6. In a bowl, add the egg yolks and with an electric mixer, beat on high speed until thick and lemon colored.
7. Add the egg yolks into the rice mixture and stir well.
8. In another bowl, add the egg whites and beat until stiff peaks form.
9. Fold 1/3 of the beaten egg whites into rice mixture.
10. Gently, fold in the remaining egg whites.
11. Place the rice mixture into an ungreased 1-1/2-quart casserole dish.
12. Cook in the oven for about 45-60 minutes.
13. Remove from the oven and serve immediately.

Ketogenic Soufflé

🥣 Prep Time: 10 mins
🕒 Total Time: 50 mins

Servings per Recipe: 6
Calories 477.1
Fat 42.8g
Cholesterol 282.8mg
Sodium 634.3mg
Carbohydrates 3.7g
Protein 19.7g

Ingredients

- 5 eggs
- 1/2 C. heavy cream
- 1/4 C. grated Parmesan cheese
- 1/2 tsp prepared mustard
- 1/4 tsp salt
- 1/4 tsp ground black pepper
- 1/2 lb. cheddar cheese, cut into about 1-inch pieces
- 11 oz. cream cheese, cut into about 1-inch pieces

Directions

1. Set your oven to 375 degrees F before doing anything else and grease a large soufflé dish.
2. In a blender, add the eggs, Parmesan, cream, mustard, salt and black pepper and pulse until smooth.
3. While the motor is running, slowly add the cheddar and pulse until well combined.
4. While the motor is running, slowly add the cream cheese and pulse until well combined.
5. Place the mixture into the prepared soufflé dish evenly.
6. Cook in the oven for about 40-50 minutes.

SOUFFLÉ Bites

🥣 Prep Time: 30 mins
🕐 Total Time: 1 hr 15 mins

Servings per Recipe: 2
Calories	212.5
Fat	13.9g
Cholesterol	123.5mg
Sodium	96.5mg
Carbohydrates	15.2g
Protein	3.2g

Ingredients

2 tbsp unsalted butter, cut into pieces, more
unsalted butter, for the ramekins
granulated sugar, for dusting
1 tbsp water
1/2 tsp espresso powder
2 oz. bittersweet chocolate, finely chopped
1 pinch table salt
1 large egg, separated and at room temperature
1/4 C. confectioners' sugar

Directions

1. Set your oven to 400 degrees F before doing anything else.
2. Lightly, grease 2 (6-oz.) ramekins with some butter and dust with granulated sugar, tapping out excess.
3. Arrange the ramekins onto a small baking sheet.
4. In a small bowl, mix together the espresso powder and water.
5. Keep aside until the coffee is dissolved, stirring occasionally.
6. In a microwave-safe bowl, add the chocolate and butter and microwave until melted completely.
7. Remove from the microwave and beat the mixture until glossy and smooth.
8. Stir in the coffee mixture and salt.
9. Add the egg yolks, one at a time, beating continuously until well combined.
10. Add about 1/3 of the confectioners' sugar and beat until smooth.
11. In a medium bowl, add the egg whites and with an electric mixer, beat on medium-high speed until foamy and they're just beginning to hold soft peaks.
12. Increase the speed to high and slowly, add the remaining confectioners' sugar, beating continuously until firm peaks are formed.

13. Place about 1/4 of the beaten whites into the chocolate mixture and beat until well combined.
14. Gently fold in the remaining whites.
15. Transfer the mixture into the prepared ramekins evenly.
16. Arrange the ramekins onto a baking sheet and cook in the oven for about 15 minute.
17. Remove from the oven and serve immediately.

SWISS
Chocolate Soufflé

Prep Time: 1 hr
Total Time: 1 hr 30 mins

Servings per Recipe: 6
Calories 368.6
Fat 30.6g
Cholesterol 138.2mg
Sodium 172.9mg
Carbohydrates 27.5g
Protein 11.2g

Ingredients

2 tbsp unsalted butter
2 tbsp all-purpose flour
1 C. whole milk
8 oz. toblerone chocolate, dark chocolate
1 oz. unsweetened chocolate, chopped
3 tbsp honey
4 large eggs, separated
1/4 tsp salt
1 tbsp sugar
sliced almonds
powdered sugar

Directions

1. Grease 6 (1 1/4-C.) soufflé dishes and dust each with some sugar.
2. Arrange the soufflé dishes onto a large baking sheet.
3. In a heavy medium pan, melt the butter over medium heat.
4. stir in the flour and cook for about 2 minutes, beating continuously.
5. Increase the heat to medium-high.
6. Slowly, add the milk, beating continuously.
7. Cook for about 1 minute, beating continuously.
8. Remove from the heat and add honey, 6 oz. of the toblerone chocolate and unsweetened chocolate, beating continuously until melted and smooth.
9. Transfer the mixture into a large bowl and keep aside at room temperature to cool completely, stirring occasionally.
10. Set your oven to 450 degrees F.
11. Add the yolks into the chocolate mixture and beat until well combined.
12. In another bowl, add the egg whites and salt and beat until soft peaks form.
13. Add 1 tbsp of the sugar and beat until stiff and glossy.
14. Fold 1/4 of the whipped egg whites into chocolate mixture.

15. Gently fold in remaining egg whites.
16. Divide half of the mixture into the prepared soufflé dishes and top with 2 oz. of the chopped chocolate evenly.
17. Place the remaining mixture over chocolate in each dish and sprinkle with the almonds.
18. Cook in the oven for about 17 minutes.
19. Remove from the oven and serve immediately with a sifting of the powdered sugar.

CHINESE
Soufflé

🥣 Prep Time: 15 mins
🕐 Total Time: 4 hrs 15 mins

Servings per Recipe: 6
Calories   324.8
Fat   16.3g
Cholesterol   115.8mg
Sodium   22.2mg
Carbohydrates   43.6g
Protein   3.1g

Ingredients

1 1/4 C. orange juice (preferably from concentrate, thawed and diluted)
1 (1 tbsp) envelope unflavored gelatin
1 C. sugar
2 large egg yolks
1 1/2 tbsp fresh lemon juice
1 C. heavy cream
1/2 C. canned mandarin orange section

Directions

1. For the custard: in a small bowl, dissolve the gelatin into orange juice and keep aside to let the gelatin soften.
2. In a small, heavy-bottomed pan, mix together the remaining orange juice, sugar and egg yolks over medium heat and cook until mixture becomes slightly thick, stirring continuously.
3. Add the softened gelatin mixture and lemon juice and stir to combine well.
4. Transfer the custard into a clean bowl and arrange in a large bowl of ice bath to cool, stirring occasionally.
5. In another bowl, add the heavy cream and with an electric whisk, beat until soft peaks form.
6. Gently, fold some whipped cream into the cooled custard.
7. Now, fold in remaining whipped cream into the cooled custard.
8. In the bottom of 6 (5-oz.) fluted plastic dessert molds, arrange 3-4 of the mandarin orange sections.
9. now, place the custard mixture over orange sections evenly.
10. Arrange the molds onto a baking sheet and with a plastic wrap, cover the molds.
11. Refrigerate to chill for at least 4 hours to overnight before serving.
12. Carefully unmold and serve.

Soufflé in its Simplest

Prep Time: 1 hr
Total Time: 1 hr 30 mins

Servings per Recipe: 3
Calories   330.6
Fat   21.2g
Cholesterol   175.3mg
Sodium   1365.2mg
Carbohydrates   17.9g
Protein   16.9g

Ingredients

2 slices bread, trimmed
1 tbsp butter
1 C. cheese, grated
2 eggs, beaten
1 1/2 C. milk
1 tsp salt
1 tsp pepper

Directions

1. Grease a deep baking dish with some melted butter.
2. Spread the butter onto both sides of the bread slices.
3. In a bowl, add the milk and eggs and beat until well combined.
4. Arrange the buttered bread slices in the bottom of the prepared baking dish and sprinkle with the cheese.
5. Place the egg mixture over the cheese and sprinkle with the salt and pepper.
6. Keep aside for about 1 hour.
7. Set your oven to 350 degrees F.
8. arrange the baking dish in a large roasting pan.
9. In the roasting pan, add enough water to come half way through of the baking dish.
10. Cook in the oven for about 30 minutes.

CHIPOTLE
Soufflé

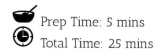

Prep Time: 5 mins
Total Time: 25 mins

Servings per Recipe: 4
Calories   136.7
Fat   4.7g
Cholesterol   186.0mg
Sodium   72.0mg
Carbohydrates   17.9g
Protein   6.3g

Ingredients

4 eggs
10 oz. Simply Potatoes Diced Potatoes with Onion
8 oz. cheddar cheese, shredded
1/4 C. honey

2 chipotle peppers, pulverized

Directions

1. In a small microwave-safe container, add the honey and pulverized chipotle peppers and microwave until honey is melted.
2. Keep aside for a few hours.
3. Through a trainer, strain the larger pieces of chipotle pepper.
4. Set your oven to 350 degrees F and grease 4 ramekins.
5. In a bowl, add the potatoes and eggs and with an immersion blender, blend until well combined.
6. Add the cheddar and stir to combine.
7. Divide the mixture into the prepared ramekins evenly.
8. Cook in the oven for about 20 minutes.

Maple Soufflé

Prep Time: 24 hr 2
Total Time: 24 hrs 50 mins

Servings per Recipe: 8
Calories   752.2
Fat   55.1g
Cholesterol   377.3mg
Sodium   524.3mg
Carbohydrates   51.8g
Protein   14.8g

Ingredients

- 4 -5 medium croissants (baked)
- 8 oz. cream cheese, softened
- 4 oz. butter, softened
- 3/4 C. maple syrup, divided
- 10 eggs
- 3 C. half-and-half milk
- 1 tsp ground cinnamon
- powdered sugar
- chopped pecans
- Topping:
- 4 oz. butter
- 1/2 C. maple syrup

Directions

1. Chop the croissants roughly.
2. Divide the chopped croissants into a greased 13X9-inch casserole dish.
3. In a bowl, add the butter, cream cheese and 1/3 C. of the maple syrup ad mix until well combined.
4. In another large bowl, add the eggs, 1/2 C. of the maple syrup and half-and-half and beat until well combined.
5. Place the butter mixture over the chopped croissants evenly and top with the egg mixture.
6. Sprinkle with the cinnamon and refrigerate, covered overnight.
7. Set your oven to 350 degrees F.
8. Uncover the casserole dish and cook in the oven for about 45-50 minutes.
9. Remove from the oven and keep onto a ire rack for about 5-10 minutes.
10. Meanwhile, for the sauce: in small pan, add 1/2 C. of the butter and 1/2 C. of the maple syrup and cook until heated through.
11. Remove from the heat and pour over the sauce over the warm soufflé evenly.
12. Serve with a topping of the powdered sugar and pecans.

BIG APPLE
Soufflé

Prep Time: 15 mins
Total Time: 55 mins

Servings per Recipe: 8
Calories   254.0
Fat   3.4g
Cholesterol   1.2mg
Sodium   304.3mg
Carbohydrates   46.8g
Protein   10.6g

Ingredients

1 C. all-purpose flour
2 tbsp all-purpose flour
3 tbsp sugar
1/2 tsp salt
1/2 tsp cinnamon
2 C. fat free egg substitute
2 C. skim milk

1 tsp vanilla extract
2 tbsp unsalted margarine
6 apples, peeled and sliced thin
3 tbsp light brown sugar, firmly packed

Directions

1. Set your oven to 425 degrees F before doing anything else.
2. In a large bowl, mix together the flour, sugar, cinnamon and salt.
3. Make a well in the center of flour mixture.
4. Add the milk, egg substitute and vanilla in the well and beat until well combined.
5. In a 13x9-inch baking dish, add the margarine.
6. Place the baking dish in the oven for about 3 minutes.
7. Add the apples and gently, stir to coat.
8. Cook in the oven for about 5 minutes.
9. Place the egg mixture over the apples evenly and sprinkle with the brown sugar.
10. Cook in the oven for about 5 minutes.
11. Remove from the oven and serve immediately.

Western European Soufflé

Prep Time: 20 mins
Total Time: 40 mins

Servings per Recipe: 4
Calories   361.3
Fat   19.4g
Cholesterol   83.1mg
Sodium   382.0mg
Carbohydrates   19.8g
Protein   26.3g

Ingredients

20 g butter
1 leek, sliced
20 g butter, extra
1/4 C. flour
1/3 C. water
375 ml carnation light & creamy evaporated milk
2 tbsp chopped parsley
210 g salmon, drained and flaked
salt & pepper
1/4 C. grated Parmesan cheese
6 egg whites

Directions

1. Set your oven to 390 degrees F before doing anything else and grease a 4 (1-C.) soufflé dishes.
2. In a pan, melt the butter and cook the leek for about 5 minutes.
3. Transfer the leek into a bowl and keep aside.
4. In the same pan, melt the extra butter.
5. Stir in the flour and water until smooth paste is formed.
6. Stir in the evaporated milk and bring to boil stirring continuously.
7. Remove from the heat and stir in the salmon, Parmesan, leek, parsley, salt and pepper.
8. Ina small bowl, add the egg whites and beat until stiff peaks form.
9. Fold the whipped egg whites into the soufflé mixture.
10. Divide the mixture into the prepared soufflé dishes evenly.
11. Cook in the oven for about 20 minutes.

BRAZILIAN
Fruit Soufflé

Prep Time: 15 mins
Total Time: 30 mins

Servings per Recipe: 4
Calories   140.9
Fat   1.3g
Cholesterol   52.4mg
Sodium   82.5mg
Carbohydrates   29.8g
Protein   4.0g

Ingredients

butter-flavored cooking spray
5 tbsp sugar
2 bananas
1 tbsp fresh lime juice
1 large egg yolk

3 large egg whites
1 pinch salt

Directions

1. Set your oven to 400 degrees F before doing anything else and arrange a rack in the center of the oven.
2. Lightly, grease a 4 (1-C.) ramekins with cooking spray.
3. Dust each raekin with 1/2 tablespoon of sugar
4. Shake and roll each ramekin to coat the bottom and sides evenly.
5. In a food processor, add the bananas, egg yolk, lime juice and 2 tbsp of the sugar and pulse until smooth.
6. Transfer the pureed mixture into a large bowl.
7. In a glass bowl, add the egg whites with a pinch of salt and beat until soft peaks form.
8. Add remaining 1 tbsp of the sugar and beat until glossy and firm.
9. With a rubber spatula, fold 1/4 the whipped whites into the banana mixture.
10. Now, gently fold in the remaining whites.
11. Divide the mixture into the prepared ramekins evenly and tap them lightly on a counter top to remove the air bubble.
12. Arrange ramekins onto a baking sheet and cook in the oven for about 15 minutes.
13. Remove from the oven and serve immediately.

How to Make a Soufflé

Prep Time: 10 mins
Total Time: 35 mins

Servings per Recipe: 6
Calories	272.1
Fat	14.5g
Cholesterol	109.0mg
Sodium	692.8mg
Carbohydrates	21.6g
Protein	13.8g

Ingredients

- 2 tbsp butter
- 3 medium sweet onions, chopped
- 5 slices fresh bread, cut into cubes
- 10 oz. evaporated milk
- 2 eggs, lightly beaten
- 1 C. shredded Parmesan cheese
- 1/2 tsp salt

Directions

1. Set your oven to 350 degrees F before doing anything else and lightly, grease a 1 1/2-quart soufflé dish.
2. In a large skillet, melt the butter over medium heat and sauté the onions for about 10-15 minutes.
3. Remove from the heat and transfer the onions into a large bowl.
4. Add the bread cubes, eggs, milk, 3/4 C. of the cheese and salt and stir to combine.
5. place the mixture into prepared soufflé dish and top with the remaining 1/4 C. of the cheese.
6. Cook in the oven for about 25 minutes.

MINT
Cocoa Soufflé

Prep Time: 20 mins
Total Time: 40 mins

Servings per Recipe: 2
Calories	161.9
Fat	8.6g
Cholesterol	186.8mg
Sodium	168.1mg
Carbohydrates	15.5g
Protein	9.1g

Ingredients

2 eggs, separated, room temperature
1 tsp sugar (plus 4 tbsp, divided)
2 tbsp baking cocoa
1 tsp cornstarch
1 dash salt
1/3 C. nonfat milk
2 tbsp semi-sweet chocolate chips
1/8 tsp mint extract
confectioners' sugar

Directions

1. Set your oven to 375 degrees F before doing anything else and grease 2 (10-oz.) ramekins. Then, sprinkle the ramekins with 1 tsp of the sugar.
2. Arrange the ramekins onto a baking sheet and keep aside.
3. In a small pan, mix together 2 tbsp of the sugar, cocoa, cornstarch and salt over medium heat.
4. Slowly, stir in milk and bring to a boil, stirring continuously.
5. Cook for about 1-2 minutes, stirring continuously.
6. Remove from the heat and stir in chocolate chips and mint extract until chips are melted completely.
7. Transfer the chocolate mixture into a small bowl.
8. In a large bowl, place the egg yolks.
9. Add small amount of hot chocolate mixture into egg yolks and stir to combine well.
10. slowly, add the remaining chocolate mixture into the bowl, stirring continuously.
11. Keep aside to cool slightly.
12. In another bowl, add the egg whites and with n electric mixer, beat on medium speed until soft peaks form.
13. Slowly, add the remaining sugar, 1 tbsp at a time and beat on high speed until stiff peaks form.
14. Gently, fold 1/4 of the whipped egg whites into chocolate mixture.

15. Gently, fold in the remaining egg whites.
16. Place the mixture into the prepared ramekins.
17. Cook in the oven for about 18 - 22 minutes.
18. Remove from the oven and serve immediately with the sprinkling of confectioners' sugar.

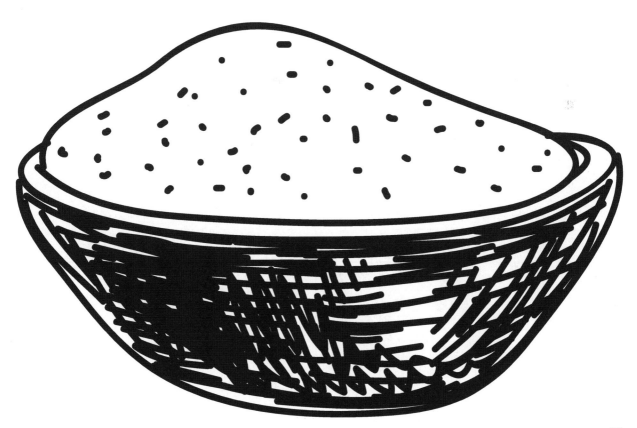

SWEET
Ricotta Soufflé

Prep Time: 15 mins
Total Time: 30 mins

Servings per Recipe: 4
Calories 123.8
Fat 7.2g
Cholesterol 112.0mg
Sodium 112.5mg
Carbohydrates 3.5g
Protein 10.1g

Ingredients

1 C. part-skim ricotta cheese
2 large eggs, separated
3 tbsp Splenda granular
2 tsp grated lemon zest
1/2 tsp lemon extract
1/2 tsp vanilla extract

Directions

1. Set your oven to 375 degrees F before doing anything else and grease 4 (4-oz.) ramekins.
2. In a large bowl, add the egg yolks, ricotta, 1 tbsp of the Splenda, lemon zest and both extracts and beat until well combined.
3. In another small bowl, add the egg whites and with an electric mixer, beat on high speed until soft peaks form.
4. Slowly, add remaining 2 tbsp of the Splenda and beat until stiff peaks form.
5. Gently, fold egg whites into the ricotta mixture.
6. Place the ricotta mixture into the prepared ramekins evenly.
7. Cook in the oven for about 15 minutes.
8. Remove from the oven and serve immediately.

Dry Mustard Soufflé

Prep Time: 1 hr 10 mins
Total Time: 2 hrs 10 mins

Servings per Recipe: 4
Calories	594.6
Fat	38.8g
Cholesterol	292.5mg
Sodium	1111.6mg
Carbohydrates	27.4g
Protein	34.6g

Ingredients

- 5 slices bread, buttered and cubed
- 3/4 lb. sharp cheddar cheese, grated
- 4 eggs
- 2 C. milk
- 1/2 tsp salt
- 1/2 tsp dry mustard
- 1/2 tsp pepper

Directions

1. Grease a soufflé dish with some butter.
2. In a bowl, add the eggs, milk, mustard, salt and pepper and beat until well combined.
3. In the bottom of prepared soufflé dish, arrange bread slices and top with cheese slices.
4. Place the egg mixture on top evenly.
5. Keep aside at room temperature for about one hour.
6. Set your oven to 350 degrees F.
7. Cook in the oven for about one hour.

SPICY Bell Mushroom Soufflé

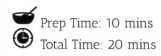

Prep Time: 10 mins
Total Time: 20 mins

Servings per Recipe: 6
Calories	327.7
Fat	25.4g
Cholesterol	160.1mg
Sodium	565.0mg
Carbohydrates	8.1g
Protein	16.9g

Ingredients

- 1/4 C. butter
- 1/4 C. flour
- 1/2 tsp salt
- 1/4 tsp cayenne pepper
- 1 C. milk
- 8 oz. grated sharp cheddar cheese
- 3 egg yolks
- 6 - 8 sliced mushrooms
- 2 tbsp diced red bell peppers
- 1/2 C. diced broccoli
- 2 tsp olive oil
- 6 egg whites
- confectioners' sugar

Directions

1. Set your oven to 450 degrees F before doing anything else.
2. For the roux: in a pan, melt the butter over medium heat.
3. Add the flour, salt and cayenne pepper and beat until well combined.
4. Stir in the milk and cook until the mixture becomes thick.
5. Remove from the heat and stir in the cheese until melted.
6. In another bowl, add the egg yolks and beat until thick and lemon colored.
7. Slowly, add the whipped egg yolks into the cheese mixture, stirring continuously.
8. Keep aside, covered to keep warm.
9. In a skillet, heat the oil and sauté the mushrooms, broccoli and red peppers until tender.
10. In a small bowl, add the egg whites and beat until stiff peaks form.
11. In another large bowl, add 2 C. of the roux and cooked vegetables and stir to combine.
12. Gently, fold in the whipped egg whites. Place the mixture into an ungreased soufflé dish. Arrange the soufflé dish in a roasting pan.
13. In the roasting pan, add enough hot water to come half way through soufflé dish.
14. Cook in the oven for about 15-20 minutes. Serve immediately with a sprinkling of the confectioners' sugar.

Authentic Vegan Soufflé

Prep Time: 15 mins
Total Time: 1 hr

Servings per Recipe: 12
Calories   363.8
Fat   14.8g
Cholesterol   0.0mg
Sodium   153.1mg
Carbohydrates   55.7g
Protein   3.9g

Ingredients

Filling:
5 -6 medium sweet potatoes, baked, peeled and mashed
1 (8 oz.) packages firm silken tofu
8 oz. tofutti better-than-cream-cheese
1 C. brown sugar
2 tbsp soy margarine, melted
1 tbsp cornstarch
2 tbsp pumpkin pie spice
1 tbsp pure vanilla extract

Garnish:
3/4 C. flour
1 C. brown sugar
6 tbsp soy margarine
1 C. pecans, chopped

Directions

1. Set your oven to 350 degrees F before doing anything else and grease an 8x13-inch baking dish.
2. In a food processor, add the sweet potatoes and silken tofu and pulse until smooth.
3. Add the remaining filling ingredients and pulse until smooth.
4. For topping, in another bowl, mix together the flour and brown sugar.
5. With a pastry blender, cut in the soy margarine until a crumbly mixture is formed.
6. Add the pecans and stir to combine.
7. Transfer the filling into an 8x13-inch greased baking dish and top with the topping mixture evenly.
8. Cook in the oven for about 35-45 minutes.

BURRITO
Soufflé

Prep Time: 10 mins
Total Time: 15 mins

Servings per Recipe: 2
Calories 308.6
Fat 18.1g
Cholesterol 126.0mg
Sodium 616.0mg
Carbohydrates 21.8g
Protein 14.8g

Ingredients

1 C. broccoli, frozen
1 egg
1 egg white
2 tbsp milk
2 oz. cheese
2 flour tortillas
1 tbsp margarine

salt
pepper

Directions

1. In a microwave-safe bowl, add the broccoli with a little water and microwave for about 6 minutes.
2. Drain the broccoli well and keep aside.
3. Meanwhile, in a bowl, add the milk, egg, egg white, salt and pepper and beat until frothy.
4. In a frying pan, melt the margarine and cook the egg mixture until desired doneness, stirring continuously.
5. Transfer the scrambled eggs into a bowl with the broccoli and mix.
6. In a microwave-safe place, place the tortillas and microwave for about 1 minute.
7. Arrange the tortillas onto a smooth surface.
8. Place the broccoli mixture in the middle of each tortilla and top each with a cheese slice.
9. Roll each tortilla like a burrito and tuck the ends in and roll, enveloping entire mixture inside.
10. Place the burritos in the warm skillet, flap-side down and cook until the cheese is melted.
11. Flip and coo until heated from other side.
12. Serve warm.

Crab & Coconut Soufflé

Prep Time: 30 mins
Total Time: 1 hr 5 mins

Servings per Recipe: 8
Calories   176.5
Fat   11.5g
Cholesterol   115.5mg
Sodium   465.2mg
Carbohydrates   7.2g
Protein   10.9g

Ingredients

1/2 C. sweetened flaked coconut
4 tbsp unsalted butter
1/3 C. celery top
1 garlic clove, minced
1/2 tsp curry powder
1/2 tsp dried thyme
1/2 tsp red pepper flakes
1/2 tsp salt
ground black pepper
3 tbsp unbleached all-purpose flour

1 1/4 C. milk
4 egg yolks
1/2 lb. crab meat
6 egg whites, stiffly beaten
1/4 tsp fresh lemon juice

Directions

1. Set your oven to 400 degrees F before doing anything else and arrange a rack in the bottom of the oven.
2. Grease an 8 C. soufflé dish.
3. Heat a non-stick skillet over low heat and cook the coconut until toasted.
4. In a medium skillet, melt the butter over low heat and cook the celery, garlic, thyme, curry powder, red pepper flakes, salt and pepper for about 3 minutes.
5. Stir in the flour and cook for about 1 minute, stirring continuously.
6. Increase the heat to medium.
7. Stir in the milk and cook until mixture becomes thick, stirring continuously.
8. Remove from the heat and keep aside to cool slightly.
9. In the sauce, add the egg yolks, one at a time and beat until well combined.
10. Stir in the crab meat and coconut.
11. In a bowl, add the egg whites and lemon juice and with a mixer, beat until stiff, but not dry.

12. Add 1/4 of the egg whites into the crab mixture and stir to combine.
13. Gently, fold in the remaining whites.
14. Transfer the mixture into the prepared soufflé dish.
15. Cook in the oven for about 30 minutes.
16. Remove from the oven and serve immediately.

Cheesy Herb Soufflé

Prep Time: 20 mins
Total Time: 1 hr 5 mins

Servings per Recipe: 1
Calories	2568.7
Fat	199.5g
Cholesterol	2162.7mg
Sodium	4925.3mg
Carbohydrates	65.0g
Protein	128.0g

Ingredients

- 2 C. milk
- 6 tbsp butter
- 6 tbsp all-purpose flour
- 8 eggs, separated
- 1 C. grated Monterey Jack cheese
- 1 C. grated cheddar cheese
- 1 tsp Grey Poupon mustard
- 2 tbsp fresh basil, finely chopped
- 2 tbsp fresh rosemary, finely chopped
- 2 tbsp fresh thyme, finely chopped
- 1/2 tsp nutmeg
- 1 tsp salt
- pepper

Directions

1. Set your oven to 350 degrees F before doing anything else and generously, grease a soufflé dish.
2. In a 2-quart pan, add the milk over medium heat and cook until just warmed.
3. In another pan, melt the butter and add the flour, stirring continuously.
4. Cook for about 2 minutes.
5. Reduce the heat to low and stir in the milk for about 3-5 minutes.
6. In a large bowl, add the egg yolks and with a fork, beat well.
7. Add a small amount of the milk sauce and stir to combine.
8. Add the remaining milk sauce and beat until well combined.
9. Add the cheese, fresh herbs, mustard, nutmeg, salt and pepper and stir to combine.
10. In another bowl, add the egg whites and beat until soft peaks form.
11. Fold half of the whipped egg whites into the sauce.
12. Gently fold in the remaining whipped egg whites.
13. Transfer the mixture into the prepared soufflé dish. Cook in the oven for about 45 minutes.
14. Remove from the oven and serve immediately.

POTATO Soufflé

⏱ Prep Time: 20 mins
🕐 Total Time: 1 hr 20 mins

Servings per Recipe: 4
Calories   180.2
Fat   0.2g
Cholesterol   0.1mg
Sodium   313.6mg
Carbohydrates   40.7g
Protein   4.8g

Ingredients

4 potatoes, peeled and cut into chunks
1 leek, cleaned and sliced
1 1/2 C. hot water
1/2 tsp salt
fresh ground pepper
2 tbsp nonfat milk

Directions

1. In a pan, add the potatoes and enough water to cover and bring to a boil.
2. Reduce the heat and simmer for about 10 minutes.
3. Drain the potatoes, reserving 1/4 C. of the cooking liquid.
4. Heat a medium, greased nonstick skillet over medium-high heat and cook the
5. leek, hot water, salt and pepper until all the liquid is absorbed, stirring occasionally.
6. With a potato masher, mash the potatoes into a bowl.
7. Add the milk and the reserved cooking liquid, one tbsp at a time and mix until fluffy.
8. Stir in the cooked leek.
9. Transfer the mixture into a greased 1-quart soufflé dish and keep aside, covered up to 2 hours.
10. Set your oven to 450 degrees F.
11. Cook, uncovered in the oven for about 30 minutes.

Mac & Cheese Soufflé

Prep Time: 15 mins
Total Time: 1 hr 15 mins

Servings per Recipe: 4
Calories	568.3
Fat	36.6g
Cholesterol	252.0mg
Sodium	678.2mg
Carbohydrates	35.3g
Protein	24.2g

Ingredients

- 3/4 C. dried short cut macaroni
- 6 tbsp butter
- 3 tbsp dried breadcrumbs
- 1 tsp paprika
- 1/3 C. white flour
- 1 1/4 C. milk
- 3/4 C. cheddar cheese, grated
- 2/3 C. freshly grated Parmesan cheese
- 3 eggs, separated
- salt
- pepper

Directions

1. Set your oven to 300 degrees F before doing anything else and arrange a rack in the center of the oven.
2. Grease a 5 C. soufflé dish with a little butter and then, coat the dish with the breadcrumbs, shaking off the excess.
3. In a pan of lightly salted boiling water, cook the macaroni for about 8 minutes.
4. In a pan, melt the butter and stir in the flour and paprika until well combined.
5. Cook for about 1 minute, stirring continuously.
6. Slowly, stir in the milk and cook until mixture becomes thick, stirring continuously.
7. Add the grated cheeses, salt and black pepper and stir until melted completely.
8. Remove from the heat and keep aside to cool slightly.
9. Add the egg yolks and beat until well combined.
10. In a bowl, add the egg whites and beat until soft peaks form.
11. Add 1/4 of the whipped egg whites into the sauce mixture, beating gently to combine.
12. Gently, fold in the remaining egg whites. Then, gently fold in the macaroni.
13. Place the mixture into the prepared soufflé dish.
14. Cook in the oven for about 40-45 minutes.
15. Remove from the oven and serve immediately.

LEMONY
Raspberry Soufflé

 Prep Time: 15 mins
Total Time: 30 mins

Servings per Recipe: 4
Calories	53.8
Fat	0.0g
Cholesterol	0.0mg
Sodium	54.7mg
Carbohydrates	9.7g
Protein	3.6g

Ingredients

1 1/2 C. raspberry puree
2 tbsp sugar
4 egg whites
1/4 tsp lemon juice

1 tbsp sugar, for ramekins

Directions

1. Set your oven to 400 degrees F before doing anything else and lightly, grease 4 ramekins. Then sprinkle each ramekin with sugar.
2. In a blender, add the raspberry puree and 1 tbsp of the sugar and pulse at medium speed for about 1 minute.
3. Transfer the mixture into a large bowl.
4. In a bowl, add the egg whites, sugar and lemon juice and beat until stiff and fluffy.
5. Gently, fold the egg whites into the raspberry mixture.
6. Divide the mixture into the prepared ramekins evenly.
7. Cook in the oven for about 12-15 minutes.
8. Remove from the oven and serve immediately.

Pepperoni & Cheese Soufflé

Prep Time: 5 mins
Total Time: 35 mins

Servings per Recipe: 6
Calories	558.2
Fat	35.0g
Cholesterol	271.6mg
Sodium	1067.4mg
Carbohydrates	30.0g
Protein	29.1g

Ingredients

- 8 oz. muenster cheese, grated
- 5 eggs
- 1 1/2 C. flour
- 2 C. milk
- 1/2 lb. sliced pepperoni, diced
- 1 tsp oregano
- 1/4 C. grated Parmesan cheese

Directions

1. Set your oven to 425 degrees F before doing anything else and grease a 6-8-quart baking dish.
2. In a bowl, add all the ingredients and mix until well combined.
3. Transfer the mixture into the prepared baking dish.
4. Cook in the oven for about 30 minutes.
5. Remove from the oven and serve immediately.

MILKY
Asparagus Soufflé

 Prep Time: 10 mins
Total Time: 55 mins

Servings per Recipe: 6
Calories 155.3
Fat 10.6g
Cholesterol 144.9mg
Sodium 419.2mg
Carbohydrates 8.2g
Protein 7.7g

Ingredients

3 tbsp butter, melted
3 tbsp flour
1 C. milk
4 eggs, separated

2 1/2 C. diced asparagus
3/4 tsp salt

Directions

1. Set your oven to 325 degrees F before doing anything else and grease a casserole dish.
2. In a pan, mix together the melted butter and flour.
3. Slowly, add the milk, beating continuously until thickened.
4. Remove from the heat and keep aside.
5. In a bowl, add the egg yolks and beat until thick and lemon colored.
6. Add the asparagus and salt and stir to combine.
7. Add the asparagus mixture into the sauce and stir to combine.
8. In another bowl, add the egg whites and beat until stiff.
9. Gently, fold the whipped egg whites into the asparagus mixture.
10. Place the mixture into the prepared casserole dish.
11. Arrange the casserole dish in a roasting pan with hot water and cook in the oven for about 45 minutes.

Pumpkin Soufflé

🍲 Prep Time: 20 mins
🕐 Total Time: 1 hr 15 mins

Servings per Recipe: 8
Calories   84.2
Fat   6.0g
Cholesterol   116.9mg
Sodium   112.3mg
Carbohydrates   1.3g
Protein   5.9g

Ingredients

8 tiny pumpkins
4 large eggs, separated
4 tsp all-purpose flour
1/4 tsp baking powder
3 oz. habanero cheddar cheese
salt & fresh ground pepper, to taste

Directions

1. Set your oven to 350 degrees F before doing anything else.
2. In a large shallow baking dish, arrange the pumpkins.
3. Add about 1/4-inch of the water.
4. With a piece of the foil, cover the baking dish tightly and cook in the oven for about 40 minutes.
5. Remove from the oven and keep aside to cool.
6. Now, set your oven to 375 degrees F.
7. With a paring knife, remove tops from each pumpkin.
8. Remove the seeds and then, scoop out the flesh, leaving about 1/4-inch-thick shell.
9. In a bowl, add about 4 C. of the pumpkin flesh and keep aside.
10. Add the egg yolks into the bowl of pumpkin flesh and mix well.
11. Add the flour and baking powder and mix well.
12. Add the cheese, salt and pepper and stir to combine.
13. In another bowl, add the egg whites and beat until stiff peaks form.
14. Fold the whipped egg whites into pumpkin mixture.
15. Carefully, place the mixture into the pumpkin shells.
16. Arrange the filled pumpkin shells onto a baking sheet and cook in the oven for about 12-15 minutes.

NUTTY Pecan Soufflé

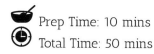
Prep Time: 10 mins
Total Time: 50 mins

Servings per Recipe: 4
Calories 561.7
Fat 38.6g
Cholesterol 232.5mg
Sodium 356.9mg
Carbohydrates 48.1g
Protein 10.2g

Ingredients

1 loaf cinnamon raisin bread
1 (20 oz.) cans of undrained pineapple
1 C. margarine (melted)
1/2 C. sugar
5 eggs, slightly beaten
1/2 C. chopped pecans

Directions

1. Set your oven to 350 degrees F before doing anything else and grease a 13x9-inch baking dish.
2. Carefully, remove the thin crusts from the bread loaf and then, tear into small pieces.
3. Arrange the bread pieces in the bottom of prepared baking dish and top with the pineapple with the juice evenly.
4. Keep aside.
5. In a bowl, add the margarine and sugar and beat until creamy.
6. Add the eggs and mix well.
7. Place the egg mixture over bread and pineapple evenly and sprinkle with the pecans.
8. Cook in the oven for about 40 minutes.

Carrot Soufflé

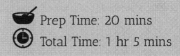

Prep Time: 20 mins
Total Time: 1 hr 5 mins

Servings per Recipe: 10	
Calories	284.0
Fat	13.5g
Cholesterol	93.0mg
Sodium	55.3mg
Carbohydrates	37.5g
Protein	4.4g

Ingredients

- nonstick cooking spray
- 5 large eggs, separated
- 2 C. carrots, finely grated
- 1 C. sugar
- 3/4 C. matzo meal
- 1/2 C. vegetable oil
- 1 tsp lemon juice
- 2 tbsp orange juice
- 1 (20 oz.) cans crushed pineapple in syrup

Directions

1. Set your oven to 350 degrees F before doing anything else and grease a 9x9-inch square baking dish with the cooking spray.
2. In a small bowl, add the egg yolks and beat slightly.
3. In another large bowl, add the egg whites and beat until stiff.
4. Gently, fold in carrots, sugar, and matzo meal.
5. Add the whipped egg yolks, lemon juice, orange juice, oil and pineapple with heavy syrup and gently, stir to combine.
6. Transfer the mixture into the prepared baking dish.
7. Cook in the oven for about 40-45 minutes.

ENJOY THE RECIPES?
KEEP ON COOKING WITH 6 MORE FREE COOKBOOKS!

Visit our website and simply enter your email address to join the club and receive your 6 cookbooks.

http://booksumo.com/magnet

https://www.instagram.com/booksumopress/

https://www.facebook.com/booksumo/

Made in the USA
Columbia, SC
15 December 2020